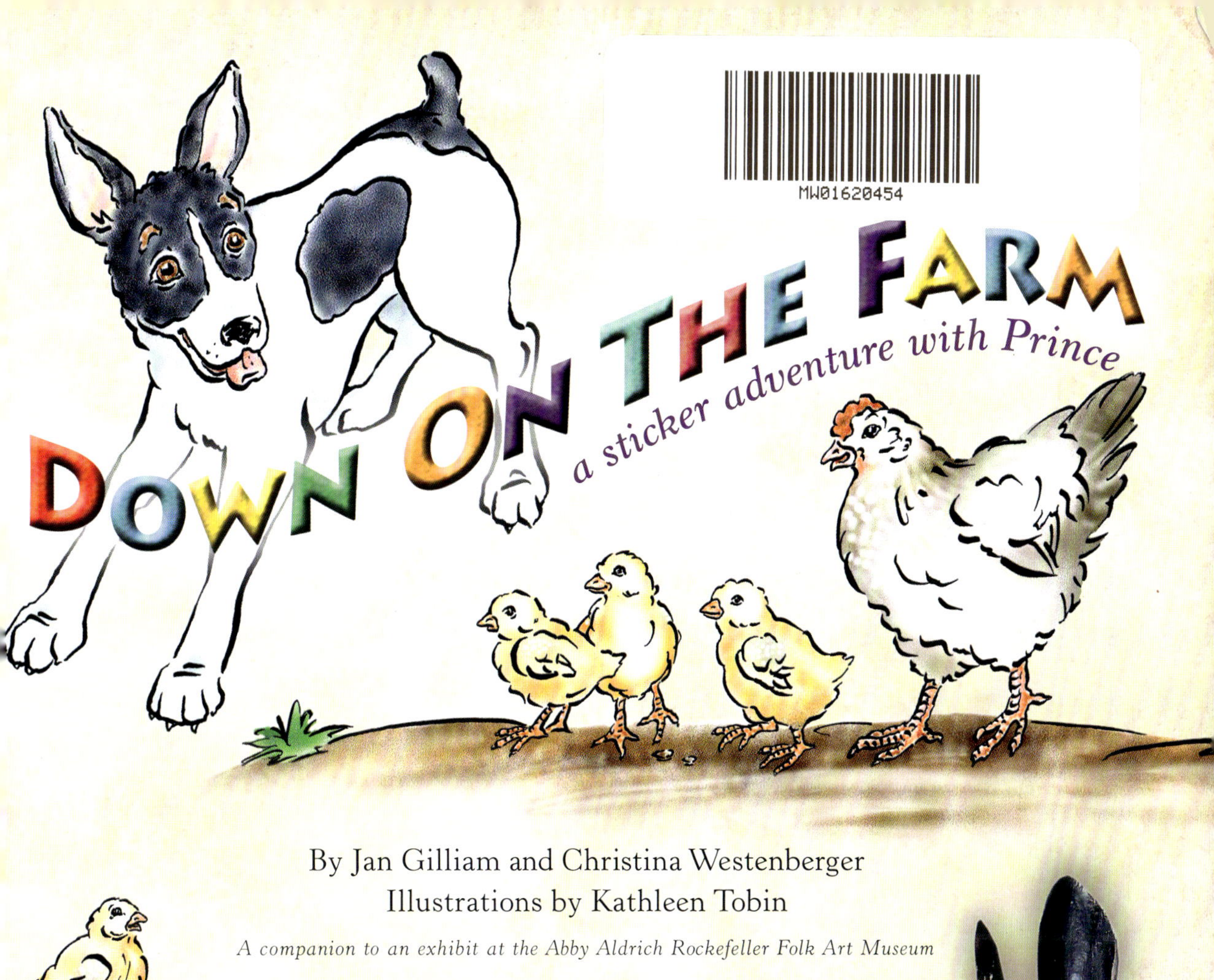

By Jan Gilliam and Christina Westenberger
Illustrations by Kathleen Tobin

A companion to an exhibit at the Abby Aldrich Rockefeller Folk Art Museum

I'm going on an adventure, and you can come, too—
just find the stickers each time I ask you!

Colonial Williamsburg

The Colonial Williamsburg Foundation • Williamsburg, Virginia

30 29 28 27 26 25 24 23 22 4 5 6 7 8

Printed in China

Manufactured in Shenzhen, China
#RP 11722.8 1/20/2022 Cohort: Batch 4

ISBN-13: 978-0-87935-237-0
Designed by Kathleen Tobin

The Colonial Williamsburg Foundation
PO Box 1776 · Williamsburg, VA 23187-1776
www.colonialwilliamsburg.org

Publication of this book

was made possible through the generosity of

Mr. and Mrs. L. D. Campbell, Mr. and Mrs. V. T. Kramer,

and Ms. M. E. Cottrill in memory of Chris and Esther Cottrill

for instilling the love of reading in their daughters,

Sarah Lu, Virginia Sue, and Mary Esther.

Our Prince is a city dog
who goes for a little jog

in the hustle and bustle
of uptown and down

enjoying the sites
and the smells all around

wondering where
there is fun to be found.

Where's the scene with a movie screen?

The lights
of the
movieplex
catch his eye.

Prince buys his ticket
and goes inside.

"Down on the Farm"
comes up on the screen.

Our doggy sits comfortably
enjoying the scene.

"I could use a change
from this city routine."

What's orange and blue and goes "choo-choo"?

"I'll visit my cousin,
a fine country mutt.
My life, as of late,
has been in a rut."

Prince hopped on a train
and rode for a day,
passing through fields and towns
on the way, and began his search
without any delay.

Can you find more feathered friends like mine?

To find his way in the country,
Prince needed a guide.

"Cock-a-doodle-do," crowed Rooster,
"that I'll provide."

Prince made clear his journey
to see life on the farm,
and to search for Rocky
who was known
for his charm.

"I'll be your guide,"
said Rooster,
"you'll come
to no harm."

Hey! Will you find me a farm?

The dog and the rooster
set out for the field.

Prince was excited to see
what farm life revealed.

"Can we meet
a sheep and a cow?
Or a horse and a sow?"

"Can we hear a duck 'quack'
or a barn cat
'meow'?"

Rooster crowed,
"Of course,
let's get on our way now."

Say, let's count more sheep!

Just then
they spied a few sheep ahead.

"We're searching for Rocky,"
Rooster said.

Rooster's voice was
so loud and deep.

"Baa," they said,
"Baa, Baa," said the sheep.
"Ask the oxen,"
they answered
and off they did leap.

Can you find more of these farmers' friends?

Our friends took the advice
and set off down the road
to visit the oxen who carried full loads.

At the Old Ellison Farm
oxen worked for feed.

Pulling, plowing, and hauling
were some of their deeds.

"Moo, Moo," said the oxen,
"Rocky left here — take heed."

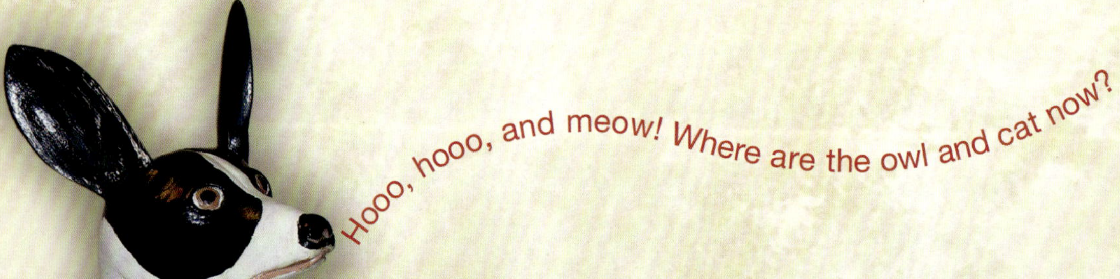

Hooo, hooo, and meow! Where are the owl and cat now?

The dog and the rooster
had walked a long way,
so they decided to rest
at the end of the day.

They stayed in a barn
with an owl and a cat,
surprised to find such a nice
welcome mat.

They woke in the morning
when the cat chased a rat.

Can you find the others who whinny while they work?

Rooster
and Prince
went on
and soon saw
horses in the fields
harvesting straw.

Prince quickly ran up
to talk to the mares.

"Neigh, Neigh," said the horses,
working in pairs,
"We can't stop to talk,
we must make our shares."

Seek critters that hop, fly, and swim!

Without help from the horses,
the friends needed luck
when the pair,
just by chance,
met some frogs,
fish, and ducks.

Could these creatures
help them finish their quest?

Prince told them his story
and hoped for the best.

They quacked and croaked
and agreed: “Go west!”

Do you see the painting of Arabella, in her dress of blue?
And, how about her fishy friends, too?

Before going on,
it was time for a break
so they stopped on the banks
of the charming blue lake.

The fish, frogs, and ducks
told them a tale of young Arabella
who came without fail
to sit by the water with
strawberries and pail.

Just testing! Can you find two rabbits resting?

After their rest,
Prince
and Rooster
called "Bye."

The next
country road was
the one they would try.

As they traveled along,
some rabbits hopped out.

Prince got them to stop
and asked them the route.

The rabbits were clever
and had not a doubt.

See the painting of the town with the bridge down?

They had seen cousin Rocky
a few days ago
so the friends hurried on,
but, wouldn't you know,
the bridge in their path
had just fallen down.

"I can't wait any longer,"
Prince barked with a frown.

Rooster found
a new path
so they soon
got 'round.

Where is the wheat and a crow who might like to eat?

They passed by animals
harvesting wheat.

Maybe there'll be
fresh bread to eat.

Up in the trees black birds
were nesting.

"Caw, Caw,"
cried the crows
as they were
suggesting
whether to fly off
or stay here
protesting.

Slithery, scaly, sly, and sleek—these are the kinds of creatures we now seek!

Just ahead Prince and Rooster
heard a great sound
so they left the crows
and went at a bound.

"Cluck, Cluck."
"Cheep, Cheep."
What a clatter!

The hens and roosters
were all in a patter.

Fox and Snake snuck in
and caused a great chatter.

Can you picture a cow, a pig, and their people?

Then
Prince
and Rooster
met cows and pigs
who seemed very funny
and even danced jigs!

A cow blurted out,
"What do cows do for fun?"

"Go to moo-vies of course,"
said the one.

They seemed
so pleased
with their silly pun.

There's another pig, see? Please find him for me.

“Oink,” snorted the pigs,
“Oink, Oink,” they cried.

“We’ve seen your cousin.
You have arrived!”

Then — Was that him? Could it be?

Up ahead on the road
what did they see?

“Yes, it’s
Rocky,”
they shouted
with glee!

Can you find the picture of Rocky's home? (Here's a hint: he's never alone!)

Prince and his cousin
were very excited.

They were highly content to be reunited.

Rooster was pleased
the journey had ended
with all being happy,
just as intended.

The trip,
they agreed,
had truly
been splendid!

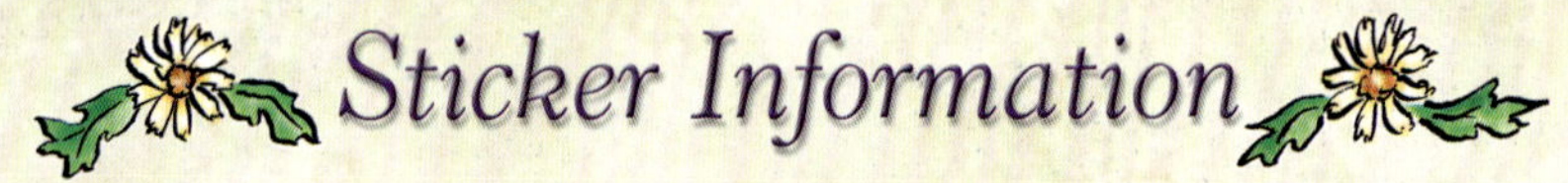

Sticker Information

1. Prince, Irwin Weil, Coopersburg, Pennsylvania, 1930–1935, wood and paint, 1981.701.1

2. Calico Cat, maker unidentified, America, probably 1900–1925, wood, paint, sheet brass, and iron, 1958.701.1

3. Wheat Stack, artist unidentified, America, 1825–1850, glass and paint, from the collection of Abby Aldrich Rockefeller, gift of the Museum of Modern Art, 1931.503.1

4. Rabbit, J. L. Mott Iron Works, Illinois or New York, ca. 1900, cast iron, gift of Abby Aldrich Rockefeller, 1931.801.5

5. Fish decoy, maker unidentified, possibly Michigan, 1920–1940, wood, sheet iron, copper, lead, and paint, gift of Merle H. Glick, 1980.702.1

6. Fish decoy, maker unidentified, Lake Mill Lacs area, Minnesota, 1925–1940, wood, iron, lead, and paint, gift of Merle H. Glick, 1980.702.2

7. Merganser (drake) decoy, maker unidentified, America or Canada, possibly 1900–1930, wood, leather, iron, and paint, 1978.702.1

8. Wood Duck decoy, Edward O'Neal, Currituck County, North Carolina, ca. 1900, wood, steel, and paint, 1984.701.1

9. Frog, Miles B. Carpenter, Waverly, Virginia, 1982, wood and paint, 1996.701.1

10. Residence of Thomas Hillborn, Edward Hicks, Bucks County, Pennsylvania, 1845–1847, oil on canvas, 1961.101.1

11. Rooster weather vane, maker unidentified, New York state or New England, 1875–1900, copper, gilt, and paint, 1932.800.1

12. Crow decoy, attributed to Mason's Decoy Factory, Detroit, Michigan, 1890–1925, wood and paint, gift of the Museum of Modern Art; acquired by that institution with funds provided by Abby Aldrich Rockefeller, 1954.702.1

13. Snake swallowing a mouse, maker unidentified, America, possibly Southeast, 1890–1910, wood and paint, 1966.701.1

14. Frog, James J. Nyeste, Pennsylvania, 1987, glazed earthenware, in memory of Jay Johnson, 1991.900.8

15. Sheep weather vane, maker unidentifed, America, 1875–1900, copper, gift of Abby Aldrich Rockefeller, 1933.800.2

16. Horse, maker unidentified, America, late nineteenth century, molded copper, gilt, and paint, gift of the John D. Rockefeller 3rd Fund, Inc., through the generosity and interest of Mrs. John D. Rockefeller 3rd and members of the family, 1979.800.8

17. Owl, Rex Smith, Fort Wayne or Peru, Indiana, 1905–1907, pine, maple, glass, iron, paint, sawdust, and glue, 1981.701.2

18. Rooster windmill weight, Elgin Wind Power and Pump Company, Elgin, Illinois, probably 1887–1915, cast iron and paint, 1957.808.1

19. Rabbit, J. L. Mott Iron Works, Illinois or New York, ca. 1900, cast iron, gift of Abby Aldrich Rockefeller, 1931.801.6

20. Ox and Cart, maker unidentified, probably America, ca. 1900, wood, gift of Mr. and Mrs. John D. Detlefsen, 1985.701.1

21. Pig weather vane, maker unidentified, probably New England, 1890–1910, copper, 1957.800.2

22. Lamb, maker unidentified, America, probably 1800–1825, wood and paint, gift of Abby Aldrich Rockefeller, 1933.706.1

23. Fox weather vane, L.W. Cushing & Sons, Waltham, Massachusetts, 1883–1900, copper, brass, gilt, and paint, gift of Abby Aldrich Rockefeller, 1933.800.6

24. Leedom Farm, Edward Hicks, Bucks County, Pennsylvania, 1849, oil on canvas, 1957.101.4

25. Big City, Mattie Lou O'Kelley, Georgia, 1987, paint on canvas, gift of Dr. and Mrs. T. Marshall Hahn Jr., 2001.101.7

26. Movie, Mattie Lou O'Kelley, Georgia, 1989, paint on canvas, gift of Dr. and Mrs. T. Marshall Hahn Jr., 2001.101.16

27. Man and Woman with Red Cow and Pig, Shields Landon Jones, Hinton, West Virginia, 1992–1994, pastel and ballpoint pens on paper, gift of Ellin and Baron Gordon, 1995.201.11

28. Miners' Train, Jack Savitsky, Lansford, Pennsylvania, ca. 1970, oil enamel on wood, gift of Mr. and Mrs. Alastair B. Martin, 1971.110.1

29. Arabella Sparrow, David Ryder, probably Middleboro, Massachusetts, 1848, oil on canvas, 1961.100.1

30. Bridge Down, Mattie Lou O'Kelley, Georgia, 1987, paint on canvas, gift of Dr. and Mrs. T. Marshall Hahn Jr., 2001.101.3

31. The Residence of David Twining, Edward Hicks, Bucks County, Pennsylvania, 1845–1847, oil on canvas, gift of Abby Aldrich Rockefeller, 1933.101.1

32. November Harvest, Thomas Buckman, probably Lynn, Massachusetts, 1854–1860, oil on canvas, 1959.101.1

33. Snake, maker unidentified, America, possibly Southeast, 1890–1910, wood and paint, 1966.701.2

34. Merganser (hen) decoy, maker unidentified, America or Canada, possibly 1900–1930, wood, leather, iron, and paint, 1978.702.2

1. Prince

2. Calico Cat

3. Wheat Stack

4. Rabbit

5. Fish decoy

6. Fish decoy

7. Merganser (drake) decoy

8. Wood Duck decoy

9. Frog

10. Residence of Thomas Hillborn

11. Rooster weather vane

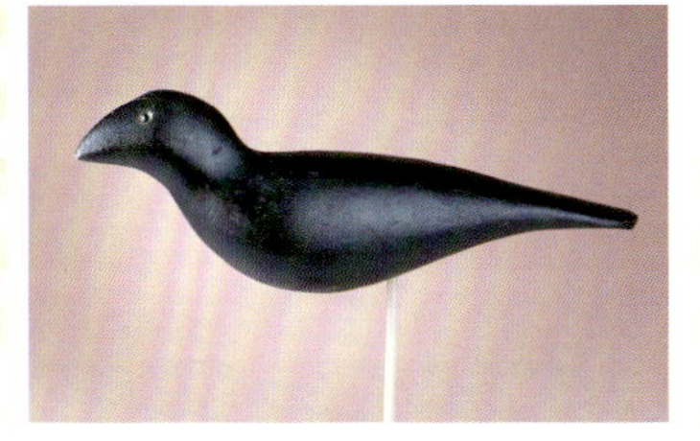

12. Crow decoy

13. Snake swallowing a mouse

14. Frog

15. Sheep weather vane

16. Horse

17. Owl

18. Rooster windmill weight

19. Rabbit

20. Ox and Cart

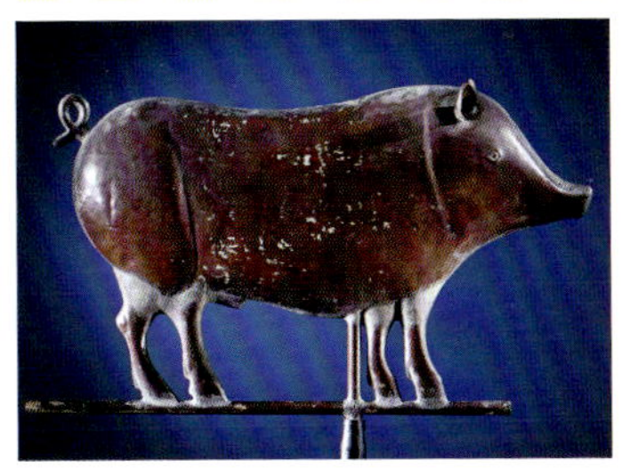

21. PIG WEATHER VANE

22. LAMB

23. FOX WEATHER VANE

24. LEEDOM FARM

25. BIG CITY

26. MOVIE

27. MAN AND WOMAN
WITH RED COW AND PIG

28. MINERS' TRAIN

29. ARABELLA SPARROW

30. BRIDGE DOWN

31. THE RESIDENCE OF DAVID TWINING

32. NOVEMBER HARVEST

33. SNAKE

34. MERGANSER (HEN) DECOY